THE INTENT COURSE

— : —

SAY YES TO WHAT MOVES YOU

BECA LEWIS

PERCEPTION PUBLISHING

CONTENTS

ONE

─ ◦ ─

INTRODUCTION

B efore we begin these twenty-eight days together, I would like to explain why this is a course on *intent,* rather than *intention.* The answer lies in the definitions of each. Intent implies a sustained, unbroken commitment or purpose, while intention implies an intermittent resolution or an initial aim or plan.

Right away, you can see why we have chosen the word *intent.* We want to be able to sustain our commitments, and not get distracted or manipulated into changing them in a way that does not serve our life's purpose.

Intents are the underpinnings of everything that happens in our life, and to our life. Whether it is an intent as big as a life purpose, or an intent on how we want to spend our evening—what we intend it to be, will set the outcome in motion.

There is another reason why it is important to cultivate this skill of setting intents. If someone else has a clearer intent than we do, his or her intent wins, or prevails over ours. In other words, we will follow what they have decided is important whether it is in our best interest or not.

While perfecting the skill of how to set clear, conscious intents during this course, you will also perfect the skill of noticing what other people intend. This gives you the chance to decide if you want to follow their lead or not. Knowing that intent underlies all action, you can immediately see how dangerous it is to not know what your intent is at all times.

In this book, you will find the *worksheets* and *tools* that will enable you to become a master at setting and reading intents. This skill can, and will, change every experience in your life—if you are willing to do the work of knowing yourself.

This book is designed to be completed in twenty-eight days. However, you can choose your own timing. After all, it is your intent how you want it to work. It is also the perfect book to use in a mastermind group of two or more like-minded people.

Say yes to what moves you and life becomes the outcome of your clear, conscious, and grace-filled intent.

I also have a free workbook for you, in case you don't wish to write in this book, or you are reading or listening to this book digitally. You can find the links to the workbook and the online evergreen course and a community where you might find others to be in your mastermind in the resource chapter at the end of this book.

Two

The Importance Of Intent

Have you ever stepped into a room to get something, and then couldn't remember what it was?

Have you ever stopped in the middle of a store and forgot why you were there?

Have you ever found yourself wondering what the meaning and purpose of life is in general, and yours specifically?

Have you ever found yourself doing something for a few minutes, or maybe a few years, and realized it wasn't what you wanted to do at all?

Have you ever been in a relationship that you realized was not a good one for you?

Have you ever bought something and then wondered why you spent the money for it?

Some results of these *have you* questions are relatively harmless. Others are annoying or expensive.

Some of them have been downright dangerous.

How can you avoid these negative results? By knowing the *why* of every action before you take it.

This may sound impossible, but it's not. In fact, it is imperative for living a life of ease, harmony, love, and abundance.

The trick is to know your intent. Most of us don't have a clue what our intent is even for simple things like going to the store, let alone our intent for our life.

However, it is actually easy to find out once you learn how, and that is what this book can do for you.

Let me give you a simple example.

You are going to have lunch with your best friend. What is your intent for the lunch? Does it revolve around money, food, or connection?

Let's say it is money and your intent is to stay within your preset budget. However, once you sit down, you realize there is nothing you love to eat within your budget.

A range of emotions may follow from disappointment to anger, which overrides the joy of the meeting.

This means you have missed the opportunity to explore a different solution for food, and the connection with your friend.

On the other hand, if your intent is the food, and it turns out the food is not very good, what happens? Perhaps you experience disappointment or anger about spending money on not very good food, and once again, miss the connection with your friend.

However, if your intent is clearly defined as *connection,* then neither the budget you have set, nor the lack of good food, would spoil that connection.

You would keep your focus on the true intent of the lunch, and the rest would fall into its proper place in importance.

Actually, any of these intents—money, food, or connection—are perfectly fine, as long as you know which one it is. If you choose it consciously, you will remain pleased with the outcome.

A clear, conscious intent for every area of your life will give you the ability to set goals, or resolutions, that you enjoy doing, and will accomplish with pleasure.

Without a clear, conscious intent, momentum can carry you down a path faster than the blink of an eye, and it just might not be the direction, or path, you want to take.

Without a clear, conscious intent, you are easily distracted, and someone else with a clearer intent than yours can manipulate you in every area of your life.

With a clear, conscious intent, your purpose in life becomes bigger than the small human ego and provides you with a path to walk that is filled with life's endless rewards far beyond your daily expectations.

As with all things, the key is first to be willing, and then to take clear, conscious action.

In this book, you will find a well defined set of actions to take to discover your intent in every area of your life, including the overall *Master Intent* for your life, which is the most important of all.

Once you set the primary intents for your life, the rest of them will be easy to discover.

Soon you will find it a breeze to discover your intent for everything from cleaning your house, to what schools to go to, what person to date or marry, what clothes to wear, or what car to buy.

The basis of this system is a spiritual one, meaningful and important to you, not someone else.

Using this system, you will know what you want, why you want it, and how to have it.

THREE

BEGIN AT THE BEGINNING

As you begin *The Intent Course* become an observer of your life. Pay attention to your actions and choices. **Don't judge—just observe.**

The Intent Course is divided into sections as if you were doing a four-week intensive shift. You could do this at the end of one year, or at the beginning of another to set the year into intents that will serve you, rather than hinder you.

Or you could use *The Intent Course* anytime you feel you need to have an awareness wake up. Whenever you use this course, be ready to shift to a new, different, bright, shiny, happy, light, brilliant awareness of life!

Each of the four-week sections have assignments for you to do. *They are important, so please take the time to do them.* If the voice in your head—which is not you—tries to tell you that they not important, or that the work is for someone else, it will be lying (as it always does).

The truth about *The Intent Course* is that this is all about and for you! Of course, we all know how much it will benefit everyone else if you take care of yourself first—if you need to remember that point in order to be completely present for yourself, go for it.

Begin by finding thirty minutes every day for private quiet time.

I will be expanding on this as we go through this program, but you may want to take out your calendar now and decide where those thirty minutes can come from.

Do it, even if it means thirty minutes less sleep, because you get up thirty minutes earlier to sit quietly. You'll experience the beneficial results of this immediately. If you are doing this course with a partner or within a mastermind group, be sure to make all these commitments with them.

During the next four weeks, you will set your intent for the following areas of your life:

Home—Family—Mental—Life—Health—Relationships—Spiritual—Wealth

In each section, you will be making *Quality Word* lists for each one of the words assigned for that week. The lists you are doing in this course will be on how you would feel.

If you love doing these lists, then you can do another list on how it would look. You will learn more about Quality Word lists later on in this book.

You might be wondering why we don't start by setting goals in this course and begin instead with intent.

There is nothing wrong with setting goals, but setting them *before* we fully understand what we intend means we are likely to set goals based on an outside picture of how we, or someone else, thinks it should be.

Letting goals be the driving force of our actions will eventually fail because we are beginning from the wrong premise.

The result of not knowing our intent first will not be what we ultimately desire. If for some reason we actually accomplish our goals, usually through shear will power or by luck, we won't be able to enjoy them, or maintain the results of what was often intense labor.

Accomplishing goals from the wrong premise does not bring permanent happiness. Goals set after intents are set become the outcome—or action—of what we began within.

Setting our premise on the spiritual awareness that Divine Love is the only cause and creator, and then acting from that awareness, will always result in increased happiness and harmony.

The work is in *The Shift of Perception*, not in the use of human willpower.

Ready? Here we go!

Four

—·—

Three Questions

To begin this course, ask yourself these three questions.

Don't answer them the way you think you are supposed to answer, or how you think it should be, or how you think others want you to be. Instead, begin by listening within, and answer these questions honestly.

Remember, *The Intent Course* is for you, and only you. Be honest with yourself. It's the first place to begin anything.

Although these are important questions, don't take too much time to think about them, just go from the heart.

13

BECA LEWIS

Even if you do this course over and over again, answer these questions again. You will be at a new point in your life, and these answers will change.

As you do this shift of perception for yourself, I promise you that everyone and everything in your life will benefit from the choices you make from your clear intent.

Be patient. Trust in the fact that the universe has your best interests at heart, and is always ready to fulfill your intents. Pay attention though, because often it will look different from you thought it would look, but it will always be the perfect outcome.

I. IN A FEW SENTENCES, DESCRIBE HOW YOU SEE YOURSELF.

2. HOW DO YOU THINK OTHERS SEE YOU?

3. WHAT DO YOU MOST WANT TO GET OUT OF
THIS INTENT COURSE?

FIVE

—— ◆ ——

COMMIT TO YOURSELF

*T**he peak efficiency of coming from pure intuition and pure intent makes conflict and disharmony altogether unnecessary and not existent.* — Delbert Piper, Sr.

Are you ready to begin? Make a commitment to yourself that you will fully do each week's assignment.

This will be the first commitment of many commitments you will make for yourself. We will spend the next twenty-eight days setting completely conscious intents that will last a lifetime.

As you make these commitments, you will discover how you feel about requirements. Just observe and keep notes about those feelings, remember no judgments, just observe.

Begin by setting your overall intent for this course.

Begin with the intent and decision that this is for you, not for anyone else.

You are not doing *The Intent Course* to get good grades, pass tests, make someone proud, prove yourself to anyone, or any other reason that we tend to do things, especially when taking classes.

This is for you. It is all about you. Yes, I will keep saying this, that's how important it is!

Stop now and write the answer to this statement:

THIS IS MY OVERALL INTENT FOR *THE INTENT COURSE*:

Now that you have stated your intent, we can begin.

Pause a moment to realize that you can expect to experience a fuller, happy, and more peaceful life just by shifting your perception, and that is what you will be doing in this course.

If you are working with a partner, or partners, in your own mastermind, please share a little about your intent for this course with each other. Share what you learned about yourself just by deciding to do this course and by writing your intent.

If you are doing this course by yourself, write a note to yourself as if you were sharing with someone else.

Six

PERCEPTION AND QUALITY WORDS

The shift that we are doing in *The Intent Course* is a perception shift. It's very important to have an understanding of perception, so let's take a moment and talk about it.

There are two modes of perception—*state of mind and point of view*.

Once we understand that all we have to do to change the quality of the life we experience, is shift both our state of mind and point of view perceptions, our lives become much easier—or not—depending on how much we love our current state of mind and point of view perceptions and how willing we are to part with them.

Point of view and state of mind are intertwined. We can't have one without the other. However, there are some generalities that we can make. If our state of mind is in an *emotion* (as opposed to feeling) then it will be harder to shift our point of view.

Since the law is *what we perceive to be reality magnifies,* then determining, and then shifting, what we perceive to be reality becomes a priority.

In this book, we will uncover some points of view that have limited you. In addition, you will find a variety of tools that you can use to shift your state of mind. If you wish to spend more time in the area of shifting perceptions, I have other books that may be helpful that you can find at BecaLewis.com.

For this book, we will focus on one of the most powerful tools you can use to shift both your point of view and state of mind at the same time. It's simple, easy, and extremely effective. We are going to make and use, Quality Word lists.

This leads to the question, what are qualities? In our small r reality they are the description of what we want in our lives narrowed down from many words, to one or two words.

For example: Let's say that we want a new car. Usually, what we think we want in a new car is determined by someone else's intent, either unintentionally or intentionally, as in advertising.

This time, instead of just popping on down to the nearest showroom and buying what we think we want, let's begin with quality words, and that will lead us to a more conscious intent and a far better outcome.

If we choose to do the Quality Word lists on how we would feel if we had our car, we might list words like: happy, wealthy, safe, calm, excited, adventurous, secure, etc.

The next step is to put the Quality Word list in order. This is just as important, and maybe even more important, than making the list in the first place.

This is because when we first make our Quality Word lists, the words will arrive willy-nilly off the top of our heads—engaging our intellect, or our thinking

21

mind. This thinking mind is what the worldview has trained us to pay attention to first, and that training has it backwards.

In *The Shift*, we first pay attention to the inner voice, the still small voice, the heart, the gut, our intuition, or the feminine principle, and then engage the thinking mind. This will lead to an action that organically grows from beginning within.

This is why we always need someone else to help us put our lists in order. It allows us to listen and feel, not think.

If we don't get the list in order, then our thinking will run the show, which is almost always counter to our true feelings. As you can imagine, this will not bring lasting happiness.

After making Quality Word lists, we often discover that we really don't want what we thought we wanted.

Once I did a list for a new car, and after putting my list in order, I realized that all the qualities I listed were really met by my walking, which is exactly what I happily did for the next four years.

In the big R Reality, quality words are actually describing God, divine Mind, infinite Love, Soul, or Spirit. No matter what you call It, the substance of It is qualities.

This awareness is exciting, because it means that as we focus on turning what appears to be things—which exist outside of ourselves—back into thoughts, we are actually becoming aware of their true substance, the substance of the Divine.

Please note: Quality words are never comparison words. We don't use them to compare what we have, or don't have now. We always develop quality words from how it would feel to have the perfect idea. We always begin from the inside out.

SEVEN

— ○ —

TOOLS FOR SHIFTING STATES OF MIND

We have a few phrases that you will encounter as you work through this course that need a bit of explanation.

DIRT TIME

This is a phrase developed by my husband, Del Piper. All lasting shifts take place within the framework of doing the work, getting dirty so to speak, by being willing to uncover, uproot, and discard.

Dirt Time is just like weeding a garden. As thoughts arrive into our thinking that do not state and represent Truth, we weed them out.

We practise *Dirt Time* as we practise *Replacement Thinking*. This is where we replace all thoughts that do not begin with the correct premise of One Mind, with those that do.

Pause Observe Listen or POL

This is exactly what it sounds like. Take the time to pause, observe, and listen. This is not about judgement, it is about awareness and observation. Observation does not lead to judgement but to dissolving.

If what you observe is not in line with One Mind, which is Love, then it is not True. The trick is to continue to stay in Truth while observing what isn't true, and then to throw Love and Truth on it until it dissolves like the wicked witch in the Wizard Of Oz.

This is not positive thinking! Positive thinking covers up and hides negative thinking. *The Shift* uncovers and dissolves.

As we dissolve what isn't true, we can hear the still quiet mind instead of the monkey mind that runs human thinking. As a result, we experience more and more of the true peace and harmony of Life.

Del tells the true story of a young man whose dream was to see a fox in the wild. He practised Dirt Time and used tools like Pause Observe Listen to still his mind and eliminate human worldview thinking.

One day while he was walking a trail in the forest, a grey fox jumped out of the bushes that lay ahead on the trail.

The fox shook himself, looked down the trail and began walking toward the young man as if he wasn't there.

Keeping a still, quiet mind, the young man continued down the path toward the fox.

Just as they passed each other, this young man had the beginning of the thought, "Wait until I tell ..."

Just as he had this thought, the fox stopped in his tracks, turned and looked at him with bared teeth.

As he began to think, the young man became visible to the fox.

With many hours of Dirt Time behind him, the young man was able to immediately replace that thought with nothing but a calm, still mind. As he shifted out of thinking, the fox no longer saw him and they both continued down the path.

Stop thinking, and end your problems. —Lao Tzu

CALM STABILITY COUNTDOWN

This countdown is also what it sounds like. It is a tool used to calm yourself down or calm your state of mind.

It sounds simple, but is often hard to do because of the many distracting thoughts residing within, and as, our thinking. The monkey mind will become easier and easier to dissolve, the more we practice this technique.

You can do this in a quiet spot, or in any situation you find yourself in, from traffic to conversations. Start with a ten-to-one countdown.

Begin by breathing in, not with your shoulders, but with your diaphragm and through your nose. As you breathe out, say to yourself, "ten." Breathe in, breathe out, and say to yourself, "nine." Continue to one. If at any time you are distracted, start again.

360 Degree Soft Vision

This is another of Del's state of mind tools for you to use. Once again, it can be used in your quiet time, or anytime during the day. The intent is to be able to see and feel, all around you at all times.

Hold your hands outstretched to the side of you and move them to where you can just see them while still looking forward. This is your side expanded soft vision. Imagine doing the same over your head and down under your feet.

This is a skill that Indian Scouts perfected. They were able to see everything going on around them at all times. When something caught their attention, they would switch to a focused view to see what it was, and then back out to the expanded view.

We are trained in tunnel vision or automatic vision. We can only see what is right in front of us, or what we expect to see, or have always seen. We miss everything else.

Using the 360 Soft Vision tool, you will begin to see what is already present. You will expand your point of view while stilling your state of mind.

As you practise this, you will discover that what was hidden becomes present and practical in your life.

You will see what was already present, but were blind to it because of your perception. Expecting to see what is already present becomes a habit that reaps practical results.

One of our coaching clients was practising 360 Soft Vision while calling on one of his clients. As he went to meet him, he realized that although he had the paperwork he needed, he didn't have a pen.

Using Replacement Thinking, he immediately stated the Truth that everything he needed was always present. At that moment, something caught his eye. He noticed that the plant he was standing beside had a pen stuck in the dirt. He pulled it out, wrote with it, and returned it to the plant for someone else to use.

I had something just like this happen to me. I was going to a client, and had forgotten a pen. Instead of being upset with myself for being disorganized, I went back to the correct point of view, that there is only one infinite Mind, and It is always providing.

I had the idea to stop at the post office to pick up my mail on the way to my appointment. In the mailbox was an envelope with a pen in it. It even had my company name on it since it was an advertisement for ordering the pen. It was perfect. It was immediate, and it was very practical.

Eight

— · —

Week One Assignments

OK, we are ready to officially begin. We are beginning with a Quality Word list for *home* and *family*. Settle into a nice quiet place and get ready to shift!

Dirt Time Assignments

1. Do Quality Word lists for home and family. You will find the worksheets after this assignment.

2. After completing the lists, find a partner to put each of your quality words into order.

No, you can't do this yourself. Someone else has to ask you the questions. Read the next chapter in this book called *How To Do Quality Word Lists.*

Then complete the worksheets by putting the words in order on the lines provided.

3. Combine the two top words from your quality lists into an I am statement. You would say this: "I am _____" completing this phrase with the top two quality words from your list. For example, *I am joyfully ordered.*

Repeat this sentence to yourself multiple times during the day. *Feel* what it means.

4. Use all your quality words to help write the story of your life as if you were living fully from your intents.

5. Do one thing every day that you don't want to do. You will find lots of ideas as you do your homework sheets.

Don't think too hard about this. Just find one thing to do and do it. Put your clothes away, make a phone call, take a walk, complete a task. Anything that you have been putting off, go do it—now!

6. Practice: Calm, Stability, Countdowns from Ten to One.

7. Practice: Pause, Observe, Listen. Do this often during the day.

8. Begin a new habit of 360 Soft Vision to replace automatic vision or tunnel vision.

9. Take thirty minutes a day to sit quietly and practise these tools.

10. Take action from that calm, still, inside, insightful state of mind.

Notes:

NINE

— . —

HOW TO DO QUALITY WORDS

The point of doing Quality Word lists is not to get more things. Why? Because things are the outcome of what we perceive within and will appear as needed in our lives as we learn how to listen, and follow the guidance from within first.

Our intent is to understand more about the true substance of what appears as people, places, and things. Since everything in big R Reality is composed of qualities, we must learn the skill of translating back into qualities the things we desire to see, or have, in order to become conscious of what is already present.

HOW TO DO QUALITY WORD LISTS

Step 1: Take a moment and list eight to ten qualities of something you want to see, or have. Use one word to express each quality. If you are using sentences, you have not come to the heart of it.

Step 2: Choose the style of list you will do. In this course, you are concentrating on making lists of how you would *feel* if you had the perfect expression of what you want.

However, there are two kinds of Quality Word lists. You can either list the qualities of the thing itself—how it looks—or you can list the qualities of how you will feel when you have it.

For example, let's pretend you want to buy a new car. Your quality list for how this thing—or car—would *look* might contain words such as red, fast, inexpensive, big, compact, spacious, etc.

If you choose to do a Quality Word list of how you will *feel* when you drive this car, it might have words like wealthy, secure, free, joyful, and so on.

In the beginning, just do how it would *feel* lists. Use the *how it would look* list as additional information.

Step 3: Now that you have the quality list, the next step is to put these qualities in order.

Why is this important?

Have you ever been at a place in your life where nothing happens towards what you want, no matter what you do? This is most likely because you have a quality, or value, block.

If you have two values that feel equal to you, your core-self will be confused as to which one to provide. Continuing with the car example, let's say you list the qualities of luxury and frugal.

Until you know which quality is first, you'll be stuck and nothing will happen. This is because at first glance they appear to be conflicting. However, once your list is in order you can receive, or see, all of what you have listed.

You need help to put the list in order. Have someone else take your list and help you. **Don't look at your list while this person is working with**

you, as this will engage brain and logic. What we want to engage is your heart and inspiration.

The person with your list will ask you the following question: "Which is more important to you?" Then they will give you two words on the list to compare.

It is imperative that the person asking not give any verbal or physical cues, or pre-decide in their own mind what your answer will be. This is the time for both of you to practice a still, calm, state of mind.

When answering, don't listen to anything except your inner voice, and respond with that answer. Don't argue with it. If you are unable to choose one as more important than the other, the person should ask you, "Which one can you not live without?"

Notice that your mind tells you that if you choose one, you might not get the other. This is coming from the point of view that there is never enough and that you don't deserve everything you want.

Since neither statement is true, just notice these thoughts and move on.

The truth is, once you are clear about what you desire to see, you will be able to see and experience all these qualities.

Each word must be compared with every word until you have an ordered list. You will probably be surprised at the order if you have stayed with your heart and trusted your answers.

How to Use Quality Word Lists

1. Use the qualities as a filter.

If something appears that you think might be what you are looking for and does not have at least the first four qualities—in order—it is not "it."

Think of the time you will save if you can eliminate quickly and easily what is not right for you. For example, you find that the word safety is first on your Quality Word list for a means of transportation, and the car you are looking at has a very low safety record; don't buy this car no matter how much you love it.

If you buy it, you will eventually be unhappy with it, and you will consciously or unconsciously figure out how to get rid of it.

2. See the qualities everywhere.

See the qualities in everything, not just in what you're seeking. Notice that they're always with you in many forms. You have always had, and always will have, each quality on your list if you just look. A quality does not have to belong to you. It can appear anywhere. All of what you see is your world.

The goal is to notice that the quality you're looking for already exists everywhere, and since you can see it—it exists for you—now.

This practice expands your concept of what the quality actually means, and as a result expands the potential outcomes.

3. Be grateful for each quality as you see it.

Be grateful for these qualities each time you see them, no matter where they occur.

Even if the person you dislike the most has one of these qualities, be grateful that you have seen this quality in your life. Know that if it is "out there" it was first "within here" and therefore always available in the most appreciable form for the moment.

4. Be, and live, these qualities yourself.

Now that you have begun to understand the substance of qualities, no longer is having the thing you want so important.

You realize that it already exists as ideas—qualities.

As we express gratitude, we are living within divine Grace. The result? Sometimes we realize we don't actually need the thing we were asking to see, or it turns up in another package, or it appears in a way greater than we could have dreamed.

Whichever way this happens, we have begun with seeking the kingdom of God First. Beginning with this perfect intent cannot help but produce in our world whatever we need at the moment. We have always had it. We have never been abandoned, nor could we ever be in the future.

Looking for qualities opens your eyes to what has always been, and always will be, yours.

Note: This chapter on Quality Lists is an excerpt from the God First chapter in my book *Living in Grace: The Shift To Spiritual Perception*. And if you would like to hear and see how to do a Quality Word list, check the resource chapter of this book to find where you can do that.

TEN

— · —

HOME QUALITY WORDS

I desire to be conscious of: *My perfect idea of home*

These are the qualities of how it would *feel* if I were living in the perfect home:

1. _____

2. _____

3. _____

4. _____

5. _____

6. _____

7. _____

8. _____

9. _____

10. _____

Get together with your partner and put this Quality Word list into order.

These are the feel qualities of *home* in order

1._____

2._____

3. _____

4. _____

5. _____

6. _____

7. _____

8. _____

9. _____

10. _____

DIRT TIME ASSIGNMENTS

MY TOP QUALITY WORD FOR HOME IS:

IS THIS CURRENTLY MY INTENT FOR HOME?

Take your top quality word and write a sentence using this word stating your intent.

Take the second quality word and write a sentence using this word stating your intent.

What are three action steps that you can take for your intent for Home?

1.
2.
3.

Take one of these action steps and write three to do's for it.

1.
2.
3.

WHAT IS STOPPING YOU FROM LIVING FROM AND AS YOUR INTENT?

WRITE A STORY ABOUT YOUR LIFE AS IF YOU WERE LIVING FULLY FROM THIS INTENT.

ELEVEN

FAMILY QUALITY WORDS

I desire to be conscious of: *a perfect idea of family*

These are the qualities of how it would *feel* if I had the perfect family. (Don't think of the family you have right now, or one you know. Just list how it would feel to you if you had the perfect family.)

1. _____
2. _____
3. _____
4. _____
5. _____
6._____

7. _____

8. _____

9. _____

10. ____ _____

Get together with your partner and put this Quality Word list into order.

These are the feel qualities of *family* in order

1._____

2._____

3. _____

4. _____ _____

5. _____

6. _____

7. _____

8. _____

9. _____

10. _____

DIRT TIME ASSIGNMENTS

My top quality word for family is:

Is this currently my intent for family?

Take your top quality word and write a sentence using this word stating your intent.

Take the second quality word and write a sentence using this word stating your intent.

What are three action steps that you can take for your intent for Family?

1.

2.

3.

Take one of these action steps and write three to do's for it.

1.

2.

3.

What is stopping you from living from and as your intent?

Write a story about your life as if you were living fully from this intent.

TWELVE

WEEK ONE FOLLOW UP

W've all been conditioned to believe the external is more important than the internal. Now we know it is just the opposite.—Bill Bryson, *A Short History Of Nearly Everything*

After completing this first week, there was a common thread among many of those who took *The Intent Course* with Del and me. Almost everyone felt discombobulated, or weird, or disconnected. This may happen to you as you begin to completely shift your perception.

Here's a short story that may help explain this phenomenon.

While I was in college (way back when) my ballet teacher suggested that we should all be Rolfed, which I did.

In each of the ten sessions, a different area of the body is deeply massaged to break down and dissolve tension and scar tissue. For me it was symbolic of dissolving the pain of past history, just as we are doing in this *Intent Course.*

When I returned to ballet class after every Rolfing session, I was a completely discombobulated! I would jump up and literally fall down—splat onto the floor, run into walls, bump into myself. All the muscles had rearranged themselves and it took awhile to live from this newly arranged me.

It's the same thing with shifting. You are totally rearranged! You will see people, places, and things differently, and will respond to them differently. Stay in the awareness of the One Intelligent Mind and keep your intents, and soon the world outside will rearrange itself to fit the new you.

It is helpful to know this is not how it will always be when you shift. Today, I get Rolfed periodically and experience none of these side effects. Soon shifting will become the way you live, and that makes all the difference.

There is a common pattern of getting relief and then getting stuck. Always go back to Truth, otherwise habit will kick in to "fix" the stuck in a not-so-divine way. Complete relief comes from Truth. It's true as stated by Jesus the Christ, *And ye shall know the truth and the truth shall make you free.—Bible*: John 8:32

It's easy to act as if you are a weather vane, always changing your beliefs and words, trying to please everyone around you. But you were born to be lighthouses, not weather vanes.—Robert Cooper

As you continue *The Intent Course*, remember to begin and end from the correct premise of One Mind.

Realize that you are already the qualities that you have chosen.

We are letting go of our collection of beliefs and perceptions that have driven our lives, mostly unconsciously.

As you do the *I am* part of your assignments, pay attention to the fact that the statement of *I am* is both an absolute being and an action statement.

It's the small things in life that bring us forward into Truth, and it is the small things that attempt to keep us locked in the prison of habitual thoughts of what isn't actually true at all.

This is why we concentrate on doing those small things! I often use the symbol of cleaning closets. When you take it all out, things look a mess. When you put it back in you throw away all that you no longer need, and a beautiful order remains. Don't be afraid of the mess if it comes. It is not who you are.

As you make this shift, some of it will feel easy, and some of it might feel difficult. There will be things that pop up into your awareness that have always been there, but you didn't notice before. Sometimes these are the things that will attempt to stop your escape into freedom.

The most important action you can take each day is doing your intent assignments.

Don't let the outside worldview and its intent override yours. When you find that you have, laugh it off, move on, and get back to it. No stories—just intent!

.....nothing to matter whatsoever. Everything out there is an illusion. The only thing going on out there, is what is going on in here.—Bill Bryson, *A Short History of Nearly Everything.*

As you continue to clarify your intent, it becomes clear why focusing on quality words and then putting them in order is important. As you do these assignments, it may be surprising how many hidden habits and patterns crop up to interfere with your dissolving of what isn't true about you so that your entire life can be in line with your pure intent.

The assignments in this course are not for teachers, as they were in school. They are entirely for you. They are designed to reach into every nook and cranny of your thinking and shift it. The quality word assignments will saturate your thinking with what is True. Isn't that a wonderful idea?

Sometimes, past habits and thoughts don't want to be shifted. Actually, most of the time they don't. It means that the end is near for them. However, for you, this is a time for rejoicing, because those habits and thoughts are not you!

If you feel like running and hiding, this is normal. Hang in there. It will pass, and you will feel lighter and freer than ever before.

As you shift your perception and begin all of your thinking and actions from Truth, then what isn't True stands out clearly.

I call this discovering *the monster under the bed.*

It's been hiding there all along. We've been careful not to live our life completely, just in case there is a monster that we don't want to "get us."

Stating the Truth is in effect calling out the monster and saying, "Show yourself, I am tired of being afraid of something and not knowing what you are."

Here's the tricky part. When it shows itself, and it will, it now knows that you have seen it and that it is facing the end of itself.

So what does it do?

It moves to the second stage of attack and attaches itself to you. It does this by telling you all the things you have done to create it. It tells you that it is your fault that it exists.

If you agree to this, you have done two things. First, you have stepped out of the One Mind and into the duality of the worldview. Your premise, your point of view, has become that there can be something other than omnipotent Love.

The second thing you have done is agreed to suffer for something you have never done. I am not telling you to ignore the problem. I am telling you to call it out and then throw it out because in One Mind there is no monster.

The *Bible* tells the story of Daniel in the lion's den. When he was thrown into the cage with the lions, he could have started telling that second story to himself. Perhaps he could have thought he should have kept his mouth shut, should have given up the premise of One God—lots of "should of's." But he didn't.

He declared his innocence and knew why it was true. The result—he was unharmed.

Del tells the story of one of his teachers, Twyla Nitsch. While visiting her home, they started talking about the sweat lodges that he was leading. She told him that she would be willing to come to one, but if it got too hot, she was leaving.

She no longer felt the need to suffer.

This completely shifted Del's thinking about everything he was doing, including how hot he made sweat lodges. She was right. We are not made to, or need to, suffer to learn.

When we find ourselves in situations where the worldview is that suffering is required, we simply don't agree with that point of view.

I know that we have been taught that we learn best by suffering. But do you think this is something that Divine Love would do to itself?

Learn from what you have suffered, but don't make it an action of Love or a requirement for Grace. We only suffer while in our false perceptions. When we let them go, the suffering goes, too.

Here's a brief story of not accepting the second stage of the monster and the result of not agreeing to suffer.

Once, Del was delivering firewood to one of his clients when it started to snow heavily. His client's house was located far outside of town on a hill. By the time he arrived, the snow had covered the entrance to the little driveway to the home.

Wanting to deliver the load, Del backed the truck into what he thought was the driveway and ended up with a wheel in the ditch.

That monster under the bed, the voice in our head, the monkey mind, was immediately present, trying to convince him that there would be no help coming for a while. It was going to be a long cold wait, and he should have known better.

Instead, Del chose to know that help is always present. This was long before cell phones, so there was no way to call for help. However, he told his son, who was riding with him, to wait in the truck because someone would come around shortly.

He stepped outside and leaned against the truck. Within a few minutes, a large tow truck appeared out of nowhere and pulled them out.

Another thing that happens when we study Truth is that we often find ways to hide from doing the work. It's not really us hiding, it's what claims to be us hiding. We can find ourselves extra busy and not realize that is the same as running away.

Of course, we know this is a lot of work! But, hey—either choose this point of view, or try to make things happen on the outside. Try for years. Get discouraged. Or do this homework and eliminate years of doing things the hard way.

Do this and dissolve the past—which is only your perception of it, not what actually happened. Instead, begin to live as Light.

Looked at it that way, this is easy, and certainly more fun! Joy filled is who you are!

DIRT TIME ASSIGNMENTS

As you work into these next assignments, notice where you appear to be stuck. During the day, are you doing the practice of Pause, Observe, Listen?

Before you begin your second week, take the time to answer these few questions. It will help you take part with an awareness, which adds to the power of this course.

If you are working within a mastermind group, share what happened with your intent and your homework. If you are working alone, still share, but with yourself.

WHAT DID YOU LEARN THIS WEEK?

WHAT WAS MOST CONFUSING?

WHAT HAPPENED IN THE "OUTSIDE" WORLD AS
A RESULT OF YOUR INTENT THIS WEEK?

DID YOU PUT OFF DOING THE ASSIGNMENTS
BECAUSE YOU THOUGHT YOU DIDN'T KNOW HOW?

DID YOU DO THE ASSIGNMENTS AS GIVEN, OR
DID YOU REARRANGE THEM TO SUIT YOU?

BECA LEWIS

Is this how you "do" life?

If so, are you willing to change it?

Thirteen

---·---

Week Two Assignment

This week we are doing the Quality Word lists for *mental* and *life*. Remember to start from the standpoint and premise of perfection! Think of the word mental as if you have a perfect mental state of mind.

Dirt Time Assignments

1. Do Quality Word lists for *mental* and *life*. You will find the worksheets after this assignment.

2. After completing the lists, find a partner to put each of your quality words into order.

Remember, you can't do this yourself. Someone else has to ask you the questions. Reread the chapter *How To Do Quality Word Lists*. Then complete the worksheets, putting the words in order on the lines provided.

3. Combine the two top words from your Quality Word lists into an *I am* statement. You would say this: *I am*_____ completing this phrase with the top two quality words from your list. For example, *I am Lovingly Calm*.

Repeat this sentence to yourself multiple times during the day. Feel what it means.

4. Use all your quality words to help write the story of your life as if you were living fully from your intents.

5. Do one thing every day that you don't want to do. Don't think too hard about this.

Don't make it something profound. Don't get caught up in the details of it. Don't worry about what has to happen next. Just do something that you have been putting off doing and do it now!

6. Practice: Calm Stability Countdowns from Ten to One.

7. Practice: Pause, Observe, Listen. Do often during the day.

8. Begin a new habit of 360 Soft Vision to replace automatic vision or tunnel vision.

9. Take thirty minutes a day to sit quietly and practice these tools.

10. Take action from that calm, still, inside, insightful state of mind.

Notes:

FOURTEEN

—·—

MENTAL QUALITY WORDS

I desire to be conscious of: *a perfect state of mind*

These are the qualities of how it would feel:

1. _____
2. _____
3. _____
4. _____
5. _____
6. _____
7. _____
8. _____
9. _____

10. _____

With your partner and put this Quality Word list into order.

These are the feel qualities of *mental* in order

1._____

2._____

3. _____

4. _____

5. _____

6. _____

7. _____

8.   _____

9. _____

10. _____

Dirt Time Assignments

My top quality word for mental is:

BECA LEWIS

Is this currently my intent for my Mental State?

Take your top quality word and write a sentence using this word stating your intent.

Take the second quality word and write a sentence using this word stating your intent.

What are three action steps that you can take for your intent for Mental?

1.
2.
3.

TAKE ONE OF THESE ACTION STEPS AND WRITE
THREE TO DO'S FOR IT.

1.

2.

3.

WHAT IS STOPPING YOU FROM LIVING FROM
AND AS YOUR INTENT?

WRITE A STORY ABOUT YOUR LIFE AS IF YOU
WERE LIVING FULLY FROM THIS INTENT.

FIFTEEN

— ı —

LIFE QUALITY WORDS

I desire to be conscious of: *a perfect life*

These are the qualities of how it would feel:

1. _____
2. _____
3. _____
4. _____
5. _____
6. _____
7. _____
8. _____
9. _____

10. _____

Get together with your partner and put this Quality Word list into order.

These are the feel qualities of *life* in order

1._____

2._____

3. _____

4. _____

5. _____

6. _____

7. _____

8. _____

9. _____

10. _____

Dirt Time Assignments

My top quality word for life is:

Is this currently my intent for life?

Take your top quality word and write a sentence using this word stating your intent.

Take the second quality word and write a sentence using this word stating your intent.

What are three action steps that you can take for your intent for Life?
1.
2.
3.

Take one of these action steps and write three to do's for it.
1.
2.
3.

WHAT IS STOPPING YOU FROM LIVING FROM
AND AS YOUR INTENT?

WRITE A STORY ABOUT YOUR LIFE AS IF YOU
WERE LIVING FULLY FROM THIS INTENT.

Sixteen

—◆—

Week Two Follow Up

There is no point in living our lives behind a facade of untruths. It takes a tremendous amount of work and effort to hide. Each of us has the Spiritual authority to choose to live our lives as the action of Truth and the quality words that we are discovering.

There is no longer any reason to be afraid of living as we really are, the action and expression of the Infinite One.

We can tell the Truth at all times, knowing that this will shift our lives to good, and never to an outcome that doesn't bless everyone involved. This decision takes faith, but not a blind faith in something we don't understand. It is a faith that the Principles found in Divine Love never fail.

It takes commitment and dedication to make the shift to spiritual perception, and I honor you for your willingness to do what it takes, despite the noise of the worldview.

Remember to always go back to the Truth of One Mind, which is infinite Love. Habit will kick in to fix what isn't working in a not-divine way. Permanent relief comes from Truth.

It's so important to remember that you already are the qualities that you are choosing. If you have my book *Living in Grace: The Shift to Spiritual Perception*, read the *God First* chapter about what to do with your lists. Otherwise, refer to the chapter in this book on *How To Do Quality Word Lists.*

Pay attention to the *I am* part of the homework. Make this in an important part of your day. Notice that the statement *I am* is both an absolute being and an action statement. Hold to these statements, say them often to yourself, and they will bring you both comfort and courage.

A very important part of this shift is calming our state of mind. The Calm, Stability, Countdown is one tool we can use any time of the day or night, no matter what we are doing.

Sometimes it is useful to take the time to do a deeper countdown. Never use a formula or make it a ritual. However, here is one way to do a countdown from fifty-to-one.

Start at fifty, and with each exhale, softly say the number to yourself. Keep starting over until you can count down to one without drifting to thinking, or get distracted and forget where you are.

Once you are at one, and in a completely calm state of mind, take a journey down a path to a stairway. What the path and the stairway look like is entirely up to you, don't try to figure it out, just let it be as it appears to you.

Go down the stairway and through an arch into a secret or sacred space that belongs only to you. Again, what it looks like is up to you.

As you reside in your secret space, take one of your quality words and feel what it would feel like to be completely filled with and surrounded by this quality. This is the process of Felt-Imagining. Stay as long as you wish, focusing on as many qualities as you wish.

Allow the qualities to become all there is, both within and without. When you are finished, walk back out. Go through the arch, back up the stairs and up the path.

This a process of going deep into Divine Feminine, the intuition, the still small voice, and really listening to what it is, and what it is telling you and how it feels to be it.

It is important to walk back out for many reasons, but one very important one is it takes you to action and the true male of *manhood*.

This is why I keep stressing taking action on what you hear within.

BECA LEWIS

Most of us rarely access our true manhood. Most of us act from the counterfeit male which doesn't listen to the feminine and instead tries to control and suppress it.

We are all clear about the disastrous results of the ego, counterfeit male, in action.

It is true manhood that protects, and nurtures based on the divine feminine's directions.

DIRT TIME ASSIGNMENTS

If you are working within a mastermind group, share what happened with your intent and your homework. If you are working alone, still share, but with yourself.

WHERE ARE YOU STUCK?

WHAT HAVE YOU LEARNED SO FAR AND THEN PUT INTO ACTION?

WHAT IS MOST CONFUSING?

WHAT HAPPENED IN THE "OUTSIDE" WORLD AS A RESULT OF YOUR INTENT THIS WEEK?

WHAT DID YOU DISCOVER ABOUT YOURSELF?

IS WHAT YOU DISCOVERED TRUE OR A LIE ABOUT YOU?

ARE YOU WILLING TO LET GO?

Seventeen

Week Three Assignments

This week we begin studying the concept I call, *What I can't stop myself from doing.* This concept is covered in more depth in our other programs, but this overview will be helpful for you.

This is the "thing" that you do no matter how many times it "gets you in trouble." It is what you do even when others, or even yourself, have asked you to stop doing it.

When we first start talking about this concept most people think about things they can't stop doing that are negative habits. This is not what is meant by this. We are not talking about the habits that you want to stop like smoking, or eating, or drinking too much.

I am referring to your USB, your *Unique Spiritual Blessing*. This is what you are, and do, and can't stop yourself from doing no matter how hard you might try, just as a rose can never stop behaving like a rose.

Yes, it often does show up in negative actions because either we don't understand who we are, or we wish we weren't what we see.

However, in its real state our USB is never a negative concept. Once we understand and begin to live our USB, the negative goes away revealing what has always been True. It is a blessing to share.

The fundamental delusion of humanity is to suppose that I am here and you are out there.—Yasutani Roshi, Zen master

This quote really expands an intent behind what we are doing in The Intent Course. We are discovering our own perceived reality by listening and understanding others, because the others are us.

Following that line of thought, please review how you are dealing with your partner if you are working with one in this course, or with another partner in your life. Ask yourself, "Is this how I deal with partners in life, from business to personal?"

Did you act and respond from your quality list? How did you feel about how your partner dealt with you?

If you are not sure how you acted with your partner, go ahead and ask. Please be willing to respond and listen in kindness, knowing that we are all staying in the knowledge that each of us is the unique action of the One Mind and that anything else will dissolve away as it is uncovered.

Everything we do in life involves a partner. Sometimes it is just a quick partnership with the check out clerk at the grocery store, and others are lifetime companion partners. Working with partners in *The Intent Course* reveals our point of view, our habits and patterns about partnerships, and that will shift every partnership in our lives.

As you review your work for the past two weeks, ask yourself, "Where am I stuck?" Everyone is stuck somewhere, where are you stuck?

How did your countdown from ten-to-one, or fifty-to-one go, or did you not even get to doing it. How are you doing with your worksheets? Bring all of this "stuck-ness out" so you can let it all go.

Notice that when you are stuck, the world seems stuck. Actually, often we look out in the world and see that other people are stuck, but don't notice that we are the ones that are stuck in a point of view or state of mind perception.

If we want to un-stick the world, we must begin within, and with an awareness of who we are and what is True.

What is True is that there are not two universes, one material and one spiritual.

There is just one, and it is spiritual. In this course we are in the process of training ourselves to look through what appears to be material and see the One, which is spiritual.

In the material, or physical point of view of the universe, we are always cycling between good and bad. You know this. How many times have you said to yourself, "Things have been going so good, it will get bad soon," or visa versa, "It's been so bad that the only way is up"?

There are no answers in the material universe although we look for them all the time. In that state of mind, or point of view perception there are only questions that lead to more questions and chaos, perhaps ordered chaos, but always chaos.

In the Spiritual One Universe there is neither here nor there, a ping-pong, or a cycle. There are no shadows where light shines directly, which is exactly what Love does. It shines directly.

As the *Bible* says, *Every good gift and every perfect gift is from above, and cometh down from the Father of lights, with whom is no variableness, neither shadow of turning.*—James 1:17

Paying attention to these questions helps you know what has been going on for you.

By this week in *The Intent Course* many people are feeling that they have reached a week of upheaval, and change. Of course, in a way that is absolutely true. You are shifting. Yes! That is what it is all about, shifting, the good, the bad, and the ugly of it.

However, the results are always beautiful and perfect because that is what you are, and have always been. What we have been doing is extinguishing the stirring mind and polishing the shining mind as discussed in the book *Taoist Classics.*

Let's choose to walk in Truth, and give up the story about our life, which is only that, a story that we tell, and often cherish.

Are you ready? Here we go with the homework for this third week. Don't stop now, you are on the home stretch for living as you intend to live.

This week we are doing the Quality Word lists for Health and Relationships. Remember to start from the standpoint and premise of perfection!

Answer these questions, as the first part of this week's assignments.

BECA LEWIS

My intent for working with my Mastermind group and/or myself this week is:

Last week, did I fulfill my intent?

What Am I Observing?

Dirt Time Assignments

1. Do Quality Word lists for Health and Relationships.

2. After completing the list, find a partner to put each of your quality words into order.

3. Combine the two top words from your Quality Word lists into an *I am* statement.

You would say this: "I am _____" completing this phrase with the top two quality words from your list. For example, *I am Joyfully Ordered*. Don't forget to actually use these sentences throughout the day!

86

4. Use all your quality words to help write the story of your life as if you were living fully from your intents.

5. Do one thing every day that you don't want to do. You will find lots of ideas as you do your homework sheets. This week, write down what you did.

Remember, the size of what you did doesn't matter. It's the fact that you did it! Remove one twig at a time and let the river flow! You can list what you do each day here, or a piece of paper, tablet, or in your workbook.

It's easy to forget what has been good in your life, let's reverse that habit!

DAY 1

DAY 2

DAY 3

DAY 4

Day 5

Day 6

Day 7

6. Practice: Calm Stability Countdowns from ten to one, or fifty to one.

7. Practice: Pause, Observe, Listen. Do often during the day.

8. Begin a new habit of 360 Soft Vision to replace automatic vision or tunnel vision.

9. Take thirty minutes a day to sit quietly and practice these tools.

10. Take action from that calm, still, inside, insightful, state of mind.

Notes:

Eighteen

Health Quality Words

I desire to be conscious of: *perfect health*

These are the qualities of how it would *feel:*

1. _____
2. _____
3. _____
4. _____
5. _____
6. _____
7. _____
8. _____
9. _____
10. _____

Get together with your partner and put this Quality Word list into order.

These are the feel qualities of *health* in order

1._____

2._____

3. _____

4. _____

5. _____

6. _____

7. _____

8. _____

9. _____

10. _____

DIRT TIME ASSIGNMENTS

MY TOP QUALITY WORD FOR HEALTH IS:

IS THIS CURRENTLY MY INTENT FOR HEALTH?

TAKE YOUR TOP QUALITY WORD AND WRITE A SENTENCE USING THIS WORD STATING YOUR INTENT.

TAKE THE SECOND QUALITY WORD AND WRITE A SENTENCE USING THIS WORD STATING YOUR INTENT.

WHAT ARE THREE ACTION STEPS THAT YOU CAN TAKE FOR YOUR INTENT FOR HEALTH?

1.
2.
3.

TAKE ONE OF THESE ACTION STEPS AND WRITE THREE TO DO'S FOR IT.

1.
2.
3.

BECA LEWIS

WHAT IS STOPPING YOU FROM LIVING FROM
AND AS YOUR INTENT?

WRITE A STORY ABOUT YOUR LIFE AS IF YOU
WERE LIVING FULLY FROM THIS INTENT.

Nineteen

—◇—

Relationship Quality Words

I desire to be conscious of: *perfect relationships*

These are the qualities of how it would feel:

1. _____
2. _____
3. _____
4. _____
5. _____
6. _____
7. _____
8. _____
9. _____

10. _____

With your partner put this Quality Word list into order.

These are the feel qualities of relationship in order

1._____
2._____
3. _____
4. _____
5. _____
6. _____
7. _____
8. _____
9. _____
10. _____

DIRT TIME ASSIGNMENTS

MY TOP QUALITY WORD FOR RELATIONSHIP IS:

Is this currently my intent for Relationship?

Take your top quality word and write a sentence using this word stating your intent.

Take the second quality word and write a sentence using this word stating your intent.

What are three action steps that you can take for your intent for Relationship?

1.
2.
3.

Take one of these action steps and write three to do's for it.

1.
2.

3.

WHAT IS STOPPING YOU FROM LIVING FROM
AND AS YOUR INTENT?

WRITE A STORY ABOUT YOUR LIFE AS IF YOU
WERE LIVING FULLY FROM THIS INTENT.

TWENTY

—·—

WEEK THREE FOLLOW UP

*A*s soon as you trust yourself, you will know how to
live.—Goethe

As we finish up this third week of *The Intent Course,*
we discover that much of what we are doing is letting
go of old beliefs. As we let them go, life becomes
easier, although sometimes a bit more messy then
usual. (Remember the closet cleaning?)

*Whenever the internal dialog stops, the world
collapses and extraordinary facets of ourselves surface,
as though they had been kept heavily guarded by our*

words. You are like you are, because you tell yourself that you are that way.—Carlos Castaneda, *Tales Of Power*

Are you also observing your behaviors? Remember that found within what you always do is your USB, your Unique Spiritual Blessing, your unique expression of the One Mind.

In the beginning of this uncovering your USB it may appear to you as the "thing" that is bugging you, or causing discomfort.

Of course, it is never negative, but when we don't recognize ourselves and see the truth behind what is happening, we may think it is a bad thing or we may force it on others rather than living it ourselves. Whatever you see and experience is always a symbol, and symbols are either the Truth or the inversion of Truth.

Once we really know ourselves what will happen? Years ago my youngest daughter asked me that question. She asked what would happen if we finally "got" all Truth completely. Out of my mouth popped the words, "I guess we would just go poof!" Well, that is probably not what would happen, but in one sense it is true.

The worldview is entirely our own perception.

When we are completely shifted back to where there is only One Perception—One Mind, and we have let go of our personality and become completely the individual expression and action of Divine Love—what we perceive will look completely different.

There are not two worlds. Just one. It is Spiritual.

What we perceive as material is really spiritual.

The quality words that we continually work with bring us back to that awareness! We are turning things back into thoughts from which they sprang.

We are not trying to put two universes together, or prepare for a future heaven.

We are shifting perceptions to see that what appears as a material, human universe is in Reality spiritual.

The quality words that we are doing are spiritual. They cannot be measured. They are not energy (which can be). They are the ground of our being, "the force," the words that describe the one Mind, Spirit, God.

As the *Bible* says: *For now we see through a glass, darkly; but then face to face: now I know in part; but then shall I know even as also I am known.*—Cor. 13:12

You are already these qualities. Claim them. Live them. Don't let habit rob you of them.

They demand action, which is sometimes a conscious non-action. They are not passive. It is not sitting around saying, "I am love and therefore everything must be good." It is living Love.

Always starting from within.

Turn around and face the enemy that suggests otherwise. If that suggestion has gotten tired of trying to convince you that matter is real in one way, it may try another approach. Shut the door on its face. Laugh at it.

Never associate this lie with a person, place, or thing. However, if it appears in your life in that form, don't give in to it because you love the person, place, or thing that is suggesting it to you.

Pause, Observe, Listen. The truth of Life is always present, and always the Reality. No matter how loudly unreality screams or how subtle its suggestion, it is still not true.

All that it takes is that shift of perception to see what has always been and always will be present for you. *What you perceive to be reality magnifies!* Magnify what is True!

You are always faced with a situation that is the same as the one that you never resolved —Carlos Castaneda, *The Active Side of Infinity*

It's time to move on to your assignments for week four. I know these assignments can sometimes feel like hard things to do, but the reward is infinite.

If you are having trouble doing them because you are feeling too busy, remind yourself that this is for you to be free. Not busy work. Free work.

Find a way to complete them in your own way. It is all for you! You have completely set yourself outside of "how it was" and that result will shift your entire life.

Keep practicing. Don't go back to that old prison thinking. You have the keys to keep yourself free!

If you do not permit the outward to become the inward, the inward will take care of the outward. —Mary Baker Eddy

As you work into these next assignments notice where you appear to be stuck. During the day are you doing the practice of Pause, Observe, Listen?

If you are working within a mastermind group, share what happened with your intent and your homework. If you are working alone, still share, but with yourself.

DIRT TIME ASSIGNMENTS

WHAT DID YOU LEARN THIS WEEK?

WHAT WAS MOST CONFUSING?

WHAT HAPPENED IN THE "OUTSIDE" WORLD AS A RESULT OF YOUR INTENT THIS WEEK?

WHAT HAVE YOU LEARNED SO FAR?

TWENTY-ONE

— · —

WEEK FOUR ASSIGNMENTS

Three weeks of intensive shifting done! Just one more week to go!

Do you see the light at the end of this? You are almost done, and the difference this will make in your life will be staggeringly evident for years and years to come.

Take some time before beginning this week's assignment to review your first assignment. Have you fulfilled your intent for this course? What, if anything, would you do differently?

One question to ask yourself is if you were totally engaged in the process—and if not, why not?

How do you see yourself today? How do others see you now?

As always, don't attach to what you observe. Remember, observation only, because in Truth you are the presence of One Mind, always perfect.

Also, if you haven't completed all your assignments, finish them up this week. It will be worth it!

Continue to be present with your assignments. You are doing this for yourself, remember? This week we are doing the Quality Word lists for Spiritual and Wealth.

Remember to start from the standpoint and premise of perfection!

Dirt Time Assignments

1. Do Quality Word lists for Spiritual and Wealth.

2. After completing the list, find a partner to put each of your quality words into order. Remember,

you can't do this yourself. Someone else has to ask you the questions.

3. Combine the two top words from your quality lists into an I am statement. You would say this: "I am_____" completing this phrase with the top two quality words from your list.

For example, *I am Lovingly Calm.*

Use these sentences as affirmations. Imagine what it would feel like to fully understand that they are stating the Truth about you.

4. Use all your quality words to help write the story of your life as if you were living fully from your intents.

5. Do one thing every day that you don't want to do.

Aren't you finding that doing this unlocks many things in your life? You won't experience this result if you don't do that work.

6. Practice: Calm Stability Countdowns.

7. Practice: Pause, Observe, Listen. Do often.

8. Begin a new habit of 360 Soft Vision to replace automatic vision or tunnel vision.

9. Take thirty minutes a day to sit quietly and practice these tools.

10. Take action from that calm, still, inside, insightful state of mind.

Notes:

TWENTY-TWO

—— • ——

SPIRITUAL QUALITY WORDS

I desire to be conscious of: *the essence of spirit*

These are the qualities of how it would *feel:*

1. _____

2. _____

3. _____

4. _____

5. _____

6. _____

7. _____

8. _____

9. _____

10. _____

Get together with your partner and put this Quality Word list into order.

These are the *feel* qualities of *spiritual* in order

1._____
2._____
3. _____
4. _____
5. _____
6. _____
7. _____
8. _____
9. _____
10. _____

DIRT TIME ASSIGNMENTS

MY TOP QUALITY WORD FOR SPIRITUAL IS:

IS THIS CURRENTLY MY INTENT FOR SPIRITUAL?

TAKE YOUR TOP QUALITY WORD AND WRITE A SENTENCE USING THIS WORD STATING YOUR INTENT.

TAKE THE SECOND QUALITY WORD AND WRITE A SENTENCE USING THIS WORD STATING YOUR INTENT.

WHAT ARE THREE ACTION STEPS THAT YOU CAN TAKE FOR YOUR INTENT FOR SPIRITUAL?

1.
2.
3.

TAKE ONE OF THESE ACTION STEPS AND WRITE THREE TO DO'S FOR IT.

1.
2.
3.

WHAT IS STOPPING YOU FROM LIVING FROM, AND AS, YOUR INTENT?

WRITE A STORY ABOUT YOUR LIFE AS IF YOU WERE LIVING FULLY FROM THIS INTENT.

TWENTY-THREE

—·—

WEALTH QUALITY WORDS

I desire to be conscious of: *the essence of wealth*

These are the qualities of how it would *feel*:

1. _____
2. _____
3. _____
4. _____
5. _____
6. _____
7. _____
8. _____
9. _____
10. _____

Get together with your partner and put this Quality Word list into order.

These are the *feel* qualities of wealth in order

1._____

2._____

3. _____

4. _____

5. _____

6. _____

7. _____

8. _____

9. _____

10. _____

DIRT TIME ASSIGNMENTS

MY TOP QUALITY WORD FOR WEALTH IS:

IS THIS CURRENTLY MY INTENT FOR WEALTH?

BECA LEWIS

Take your top quality word and write a sentence using this word stating your intent.

Take the second quality word and write a sentence using this word stating your intent.

What are three action steps that you can take for your intent for Wealth?

1.
2.
3.

Take one of these action steps and write Three to do's for it.

1.
2.
3.

WHAT IS STOPPING YOU FROM LIVING FROM
AND AS YOUR INTENT?

WRITE A STORY ABOUT YOUR LIFE AS IF YOU
WERE LIVING FULLY FROM THIS INTENT.

Twenty-Four

—·—

Week Four Follow Up

F our weeks! You did it! However, this is just the beginning. Continue with what you have started. Continue to dissolve what isn't True and live as what is!

Remember, don't let fear, or confusion, or secrets pull you away from dancing the dance of your life. I am calling you out to dance on the streets of life with me.

Let the world see the beauty of who you are!

I do have one last assignment for you to wrap all of this work into one quality word that you can carry with you as your own personal guiding star.

In this last assignment, you will take the **top eight words** from the **eight quality lists** that you have done in the past four weeks, and then put those eight words into order.

This will be your *Master Intent List*.

Can you see how valuable this would be? When you write your sentence after doing the list, you will have a statement that describes the current baseline intent for your entire life.

Using your *Master Intent,* you will be able to make quick decisions, and take action knowing that you are remaining on the path you what to take.

Take the time to do this last list, and cap off all your work with this simple way of reminding yourself who you are and what is important to you.

TWENTY-FIVE

—·—

MY MASTER INTENT

These are my eight top Quality Words from the previously prepared Quality Word lists.

1. _____
2. _____
3. _____
4. _____
5. _____
6. _____
7. _____
8. _____

Get together with your partner and put this Quality Word list into order.

These are the qualities in order

1._____ ___

2._____

3. _____

4. _____

5. _____

6. _____

7. _____

8. _____

DIRT TIME ASSIGNMENTS

TAKE THE TOP WORD FROM THIS MASTER QUALITY LIST AND ENTER IT HERE AS THE BASELINE INTENT OF YOUR LIFE AND AS THE I AM STATEMENT.

MY BASELINE WORD OF INTENT FOR MY LIFE IS:

TAKE YOUR TOP QUALITY WORD AND WRITE
A SENTENCE USING THIS WORD STATING YOUR
INTENT.

TAKE THE NEXT QUALITY WORD AND WRITE
A SENTENCE USING THIS WORD STATING YOUR
INTENT.

TAKE THE TOP WORD AND THE SECOND WORD
ON YOUR MASTER QUALITY LIST AND COMBINE
THE TWO. FOR EXAMPLE: *I AM THE AWARENESS OF
LIGHT.*

OR, TAKE THE TOP WORD ON TWO OF YOUR
LISTS AND COMBINE THEM—THE COMBINATIONS
ARE ENDLESS!

I am:

WHAT ARE THREE ACTION STEPS THAT YOU CAN TAKE FOR YOUR INTENT FOR YOUR LIFE?

1.

2.

3.

TAKE ONE OF THESE ACTION STEPS AND WRITE THREE TO DO'S FOR IT.

1.

2.

3.

WHAT IS STOPPING YOU FROM LIVING FROM, AND AS, YOUR INTENT?

WRITE A STORY ABOUT YOUR LIFE AS IF YOU WERE LIVING THIS INTENT FULLY.

KEEP UP YOUR POL ASSIGNMENTS AND LIVE YOUR QUALITY WORDS IN YOUR SACRED SPACE.

BECA LEWIS

Take some time to review with your mastermind partners, or with yourself, where you are today.

What has changed?

What has stayed the same?

Write a sentence using all of your eight quality words. Read this sentence every day. This is your Master Intent.

You have set the course of your life based on your own consciously chosen clear values and priorities, and now they can become the intents that direct your life.

When you know your intent based on these pure values, you cannot be manipulated, swayed, or distracted.

Instead, you will feel the strong, steady support of the universe working in harmony and accord to the greatest outcome for you and your loved ones.

Mastering the skill of how to set intents can be applied to every aspect of your life, from deciding what is for dinner to your life purpose.

You choose and the universe answers in kind.

— · —

Resources

F ind *The Intent Course* workbook, and helpful
videos at PerceptionU.com

Find others to support you in the *Perception Circle*
also at PerceptionU.com

AUTHOR NOTE

Thank you for reading my books! It is for you that I write.

If you like what I write, you can help spread the word, and keep my work going, by "liking" my books anywhere the option is offered. I would be honored if you would also post your honest reviews of the book. This will help other readers decide whether it is worth their reading time.

In today's world, it is the reader that spreads the word about books they like. If you like mine, anyway you choose to do this will be so helpful. I thank you in advance for all that you do!

I hope this book has helped you discover more about the truth of yourself, and that your life will expand in wonderful ways because of this knowledge.

Join my mailing list at becalewis.com and see what books I am giving away for free.

I am looking forward to getting to know you!

-Beca

—·—

OTHER PLACES TO FIND BECA

- Facebook: facebook.com/becalewiscreative

- Instagram: instagram.com/becalewis

- Twitter: twitter.com/becalewis

- LinkedIn: linkedin.com/in/becalewis

- Youtube: www.youtube.com/c/becalewis

The Chronicles of Thamon: Fantasy
Banished, Betrayed, Discovered, Wren's Story

The Shift Series: Spiritual Self-Help
Living in Grace: The Shift to Spiritual Perception
The Daily Shift: Daily Lessons From Love To Money
The 4 Essential Questions: Choosing Spiritually
Healthy Habits
The 28 Day Shift To Wealth: A Daily Prosperity Plan
The Intent Course: Say Yes To What Moves You
Imagination Mastery: A Workbook For Shifting Your
Reality
Right Thinking: A Thoughtful System for Healing
Perception Mastery: Seven Steps To Lasting Change
Blooming Your Life: How To Experience Consistent
Happiness

Perception Parables: Very short stories
Love's Silent Sweet Secret: A Fable About Love

BECA LEWIS

Golden Chains And Silver Cords: A Fable About
Letting Go

Advice:

A Woman's ABC's of Life: Lessons in Love, Life, and
Career from Those Who Learned The Hard Way
The Daily Nudge: So When Did You First Notice

ABOUT BECA

Beca writes books she hopes will change people's perceptions of themselves and the world, and open possibilities to things and ideas that are waiting to be seen and experienced.

At sixteen, Beca founded her own dance studio. Later, she received a Master's Degree in Dance in Choreography from UCLA and founded the Harbinger Dance Theatre, a multimedia dance company, while continuing to run her dance school.

After graduating—to better support her three children—Beca switched to the sales field, where she worked as an employee and independent contractor to many industries, excelling in each while perfecting and teaching her Shift® system, and writing books.

She joined the financial industry in 1983 and became an Associate Vice President of Investments at a major stock brokerage firm, and was a licensed Certified Financial Planner for over twenty years.

This diversity, along with a variety of life challenges, helped fuel the desire to share what she's learned by writing and speaking, hoping it will make a difference in other people's lives.

Beca grew up in State College, PA, with the dream of becoming a dancer and then a writer. She carried that dream forward as she fulfilled a childhood wish by moving to Southern California in 1968. Beca told her family she would never move back to the cold.

After living there for thirty-one years, she met her husband Delbert Lee Piper, Sr., at a retreat in Virginia, and everything changed. They decided to find a place they could call their own, which sent them off traveling around the United States. They lived and worked in a few different places before returning to live in the cold once again near Del's family in a small town in Northeast Ohio, not too far from State College.

When not working and teaching together, they love to visit and play with their combined family of eight children and five grandchildren, read, study, do yoga or taiji, feed birds, and work in their garden.

Printed in Great Britain
by Amazon

51861407R00079